Modern Hieroglyphics

John Hanrahan – UWW World Champion

DEDICATION

This book is dedicated to the sport of wrestling, which has had a profound positive affect on my life and has given me the fortitude to conquer many challenges. It is my hope that many boys and girls will be introduced to the world's oldest sport and gain the love and perseverance to take on any and all challenges that life throws at you. As Dan Gable is quoted as saying: "once you've wrestled, everything else in life is easy."

CONTENTS

ACKNOWLEDGMENTS

I began wrestling in second grade at the Annandale Boys Club in its inaugural season.. The late Fred Ruffling (RIP) was instrumental in forming the Northern Virginia Boys Club Wrestling Federation. I had many great battles with Mr Ruffing's son Matt Ruffing. Bill Richter was my very first boy's club coach and he'd bring Olympian, Bobby Douglas' book of moves to practice and do his best to show us techniques.

By Jr HS I began wrestling for the great Roger Rinker at Braddock Road Boys Club CAWL travel team. Onward to two National Wrestling Hall of Fame coaches; Steve Wilcox at Falls Church HS and then Rich Lorenzo at Penn State. Competing for the NYAC I was coached by Iranian World Champ, Hamid Kermanshah.

This book is to honor all the great coaches out there and the positive affect they have at every level in a kid's journey.

FOREWARD

A BRIEF HISTORY OF WRESTLING

Wrestling dates back to prehistoric times and is considered the world's oldest and purest sport. In French caves, there are drawings reported to be 15,000 to 20,000 years old depicting wrestlers in various holds and leverage positions. Wrestling was introduced to the Olympic Games in Greece about 708 BC. The Greek philosopher Plato was an accomplished wrestler. Native Americans wrestled for sport long before the first Europeans arrived. Ten of our US Presidents were wrestlers. Washington and Lincoln were considered to be excellent at the sport, both holding various championship titles. Others were Jackson, Taylor, Grant, Arthur, Taft, Teddy Roosevelt, Coolidge and even Trump wrestled for a season at his high school boarding school.

Why Learn to Wrestle?

One former wrestler's unselfish courageous determination can best illustrate the value in answering this question. Former New Jersey all-state wrestler, Jeremy Glick with two fellow passengers aboard Flight 93 (Tom Burnett and Todd Beamer) heeded the famous 9/11 call "Let's Roll", and proceeded to "wrestle" on behalf of us all, against terrorism. Sports Illustrated writer Rick Reilly said it best; "At a time like this, sports are trivial. But what the best athletes can do -- keep their composure amid chaos, form a plan when all seems lost, and find the guts to carry it out -- may be why the Capitol isn't a charcoal pit". Sports may be trivial but the lessons and courage learned through them can become the foundation to monumental achievements. I spoke recently to famed American wrestler Dan Gable who reminded me that; "after you've wrestled, everything else in life is easy".

Why This Book

I was inspired to write this book when I began teaching my two young sons (Colin and Luke, pictured left) the sport of wrestling. I had competed as a champion collegiate wrestler and had the great fortune of being exposed to many great coaches throughout my career. I had always been intrigued by the ancient history of the sport of wrestling and how many moves still used today were depicted through ancient hieroglyphics. This book along with my free YouTube Channel Instructional Series is my way of passing on to future generations, the moves and techniques that allowed me to compete against the best wrestlers in the world. MODERN HIEROGLYPHICS is a resource developed to help young kids, teens, parents and coaches better understand the full array of moves to compete in the great sport of wrestling.

After competing I worked as a collegiate wrestling coach (at Penn State, Fordham and American Universities) and won the UWW Veteran Division World Championship of Freestyle Wrestling. I also went on to become a nationally acclaimed fitness specialist which has given me a further insight into how to properly prepare your body for the rigorous demands of the "oldest sport". This book is not only from a Wrestling Coaches perspective who has helped to create many national champions but also contains important strategies and tips on proper exercise and nutrition, from a Strength and Conditioning Coach's perspective.

This book provides a valuable tool for the youth or high school competitor or coach, with technical guidance to a full arsenal of techniques which delivers a complete tactical wrestling system, both defensively and offensively. Simple and complex moves are broken down, described precisely and illustrated with over 700 sequential photographs dedicated to depicting over 50 maneuvers.

Muscular Strength Training, Energy System Conditioning, Flexibility, Diet and Optimal Body Composition are all issues and element that must be addressed to be a successful wrestler. All are addressed in this publication. The Mindset of a Champion is a philosophy that is also discussed. Champions have traits in common that can be honed and developed, to help you become your best and be fully prepared for the stress, triumph and adversities that come with competition.

Part I TAKEDOWNS

John Hanrahan of Penn State takes a single leg against John Reich of the US Naval Academy.

* Neutral Positioning

Proper stance and positioning allows a wrestler to set up for offensive shots, while at the same time provides a defensive barrier against the opponents attacks. Key elements include, keeping knees bent with the elbows in, weight shifting evenly, never crossing your legs or ankles as you circle and maneuvering for superior head position and for an angle of advantage to attack. Circling or advancing, not backing up, dictating the movement and the tempo. A square stance provides stability and a great defensive base. A staggered stance (with one leg forward) allows you to keep the back leg cocked and ready to trigger a penetration shot for a leg attack.

In a staggered stance never reach with your Lead Leg side arm. Use that lead leg arm to always protect that lead leg which is vulnerable to attack if your arm becomes extended. Reaching with your Lead Leg side arm leaves the Lead Leg defenseless.

Keeping the weight on the back leg leaves you continuously set for your shots and also allows you to quickly pull back your Lead Leg in defense of an incoming opponent's shot.

Move & Shoot Setting Opponent. Dictate & Lead the Movement. Keep weight on the

Back Foot - Cocked & Loaded Ready to Spring a Penetration Step at any moment.

Lead Leg Arm Protection

Use the forward leg arm to protect against penetration of your Lead Leg. You should never extend or reach with your Lead Leg Arm or you become vulnerable to an easy attack. Keep your elbow in and be ready to use the arm as a Down Blocker on an opponent's attack or as an attack arm when coming in with deep penetration on an attack.

* Arm & Head Positioning

Head Position

A key component in gaining a tactical edge is Head Positioning. The wrestler who keeps the lower level of Head Positioning while also maintaining stance will hold the edge both offensively and defensively. Keep inside control and constantly pressure back against your opponents center of balance. If you find yourself losing the battle of Head Positioning use the back of your head to come up and regain a superior position.

Arm Positions - Antagonist Arm on Back Leg Side Reach & The Shot Protector Arm on the Front Leg Side

* Hand Fighting

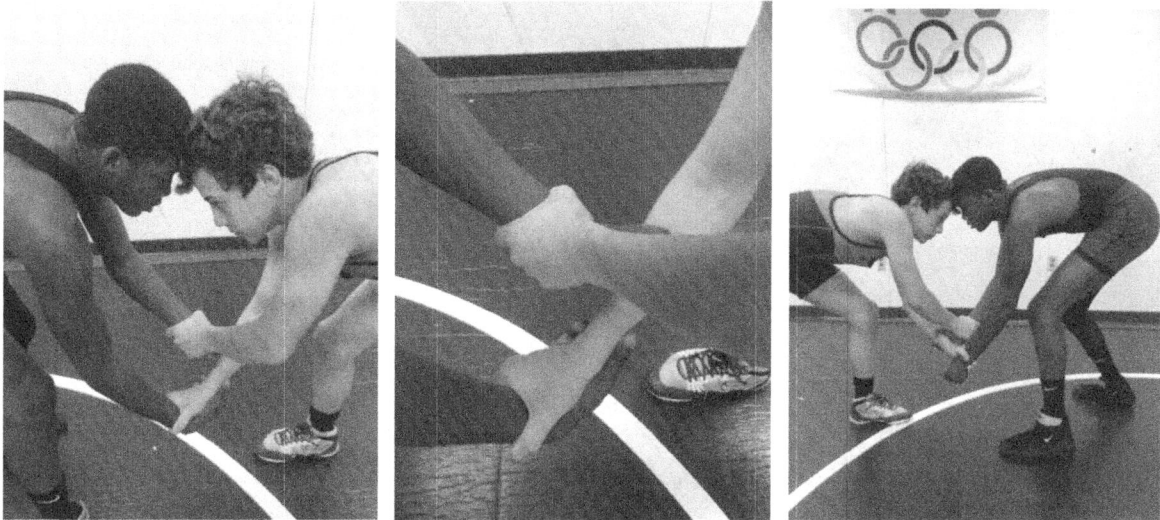

Another key component for a successful attack is the ability to clear your opponent's arms. This is called the battle of Hand Fighting. Using two on one and single grip tactics you can create movement and dictate your opponent's movement looking for arm drags and arm clears. While at the same time remembering the battle of Head Position and Stance position. Use Hand Fighting grips to move and set your opponent. Creating offensive angles, utilizing Hand Fighting, Head Positioning and maintaining Stance.

* Arm Drags & Arm Clears

Arm drags are a very effective way to clear your opponent's arms and to pull yourself inward for a close body attack. A downward Chopping Drag is also effective when your opponent comes in with a tight grip. Chop with your fore arm downward then catching him by hooking his tricep with your opposite arm, pull across the body, get your angle and come behind, securing the hips.

A great way to set for the drag is to give your opponent a head snap, when he reaches up catch and feed that arm across the body catching the tricep with a hook with your opposite arm then coming around for control.

Drags - Clear your opponents arm with a sweeping motion feeding it across the body and hooking it with your opposite arm to pull your opponent by.

Posts - when a man reaching catch his arm above the elbow, posting it upward just enough to clear for an avenue of unimpeded attack towards his legs.

Arm Drag to a Single

An arm drag will also set and clear the way for a straight Single Leg shot.

When the opponent reaches catch the arm by swinging your arm in a circular motion, and take it across the body - as the arm is swung across reach deep with the opposite arm, hooking deep behind the upper tricep. Pull the arm across while stepping in and penetrating deep with a Head Inside Single Leg.

Clears - Simply catch your opponent reaching and pressure his arm across his body so that you have a gained a momentary angle of clear unimpeded attack. Be ready to take your shot in immediately upon clearing the arm, always be setting your back foot to spring a penetration step so that you are ready to fire when you get your clear route of attack.

Use two on one grips to move and set your opponent, creating offensive angles. Remember to get to your opponent's body you must first find a way to clear his head and arms.

* Set Ups - Head Snaps, Push & Pulls

Using your Back Leg Arm as the antagonist you can safely reach with your Back Leg Arm and create movement by Pushing and Pulling. Never hang or hold a collar tie - rather use to create a pushing or pulling movement that will dictate a reaction and allow you a clear shot to your opponent's legs. The Lead Leg Arm must always continue to protect the Lead Leg, keeping the elbow in.

Your opponent's reaction to a wrist pull can be the perfect set up to a Double or Single Leg.

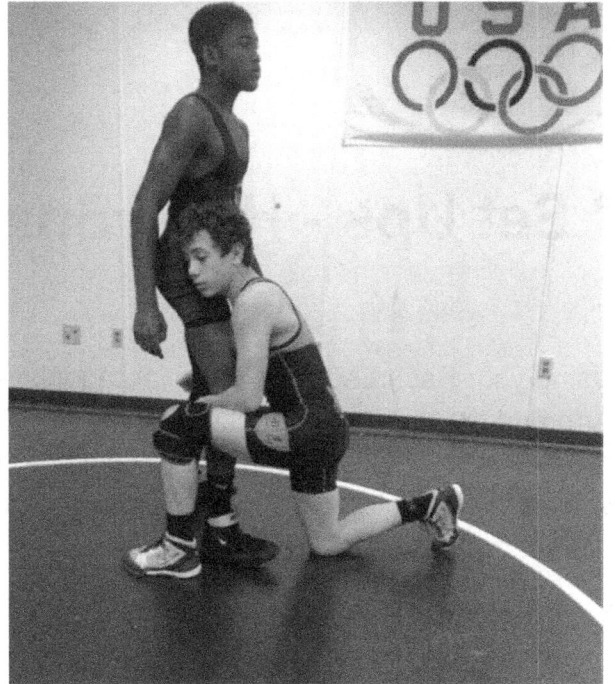

Your opponent's reaction to a Head Snap can be the perfect set up for a double or single Leg shot. - Snap the Head and the man will rear back, with your back leg set to spring a penetration shot you pull the trigger as you release the snap letting his head come upward and creating an avenue of attack.

A quick snap also sets you up for your arm drag, Snaps performed correctly can open up all kinds of offensive shots.

* Double Leg Penetration Attacks

The key to a successful penetration shot is covering distance - shooting through your opponent's legs. You must aim to shoot three-times the distance of where your opponent's legs are at the start of your shot. Your target is fluid not stationary - your opponents legs will be sprawling as you come in thus you must be set to cover the distance it will take to secure control.

Remember to set yourself with weight on the back foot, back leg is cocked and loaded ready to spring. Shift your weight step up and penetrate forward with your lead leg knee hitting the mat and your push leg then sliding forward - keeping the momentum and the penetration going the distance required to gain control. Go all the way or do not go at all, there is nothing more ugly or painful then taking a half shot

This Head in The Gut Animalistic Double requires deep penetration and secure hooks behind the opponent's knees. As you continue driving with the head in the abdomen, also pull the knee hooks inward, dropping the opponent as you penetrate through..

Head Outside - as you penetrate in through the legs slip the head to the outside, secure the opponent's thighs with a lock below his buttock. Once you are in deep give a quick lift and drop the opponent away from your head.

Lift & Dump Away From the Head

Sweep & Collapse Far Knee - Rotation Double - Penetrate with a step in for a Double Leg locking at the thighs with your head to the outside, begin rotating around your opponent while collapsing the opponent's far knee as you turn the corner. You can sweep a double as in the Single Leg Sweep, by using Hi-Leg momentum and by hooking the far knee while sweeping and collapsing the far knee as you drive your opponent in a circular motion.

Snap and Shoot

* Inside-Step Single Leg

Single Leg Attack with a Straight Inside-Step Shot

The inside step single is performed by getting your opponent to step away from your Lead Leg. Set yourself and penetrate with a step through the opponent's legs, splitting the seam of his legs coming in tight with your head inside as a lever, pick up the leg with your arms, securing the single leg tightly with your shoulder digging into his quadriceps muscle.- take a withdrawing downward spiraling step to dump your opponent to the mat. Set yourself as you circle setting yourself to shoot as he follows, as he does come in clean pick up the leg pressure in with your shoulder and dropping him to the mat. Always finish with your weight on the opponent tying up an arm or a leg in the process. The shot is easy to anticipate when you are the one dictating the movement you know he will step because you are creating the movement set yourself and penetrate deep and tight to secure the leg with head and shoulder pressure.

* Outside-Step Single Leg

The outside step single shot - Clear your opponents arms, stepping to the outside pushing off the back foot come in deep and tight, picking the leg up with your head positioned inside for maximum leverage. With the leg secured make the man take a hop back on his one free leg then immediately withdraw into a circular downward dropping motion, dumping him to the mat.

Outside step - off a Man's Reach with a Post or Arm Cross-Clear

* Finishing the Single Leg

Dropping Opponent to Mat

Getting in on the single is only half the battle, finishing is most important. When you get in and up on a single you need to keep leverage with your head and find pressure with your shoulder onto your opponent's quadriceps (thigh), You need to create movement in order to drop him. Once secured step in and make him hop back then take a withdrawing step and drop him in a corkscrewing downward motion.

Head Position, Shoulder in Quad

Stuck Underneath - Post & Turn Corner

Most single leg shots end up as a dog fight down on the mat. To get around and score post your locked grip palms down to the mat. Pivot around the trapped single leg, pressuring upward with your head and pressuring inward with your shoulder. Turn the corner and take control.

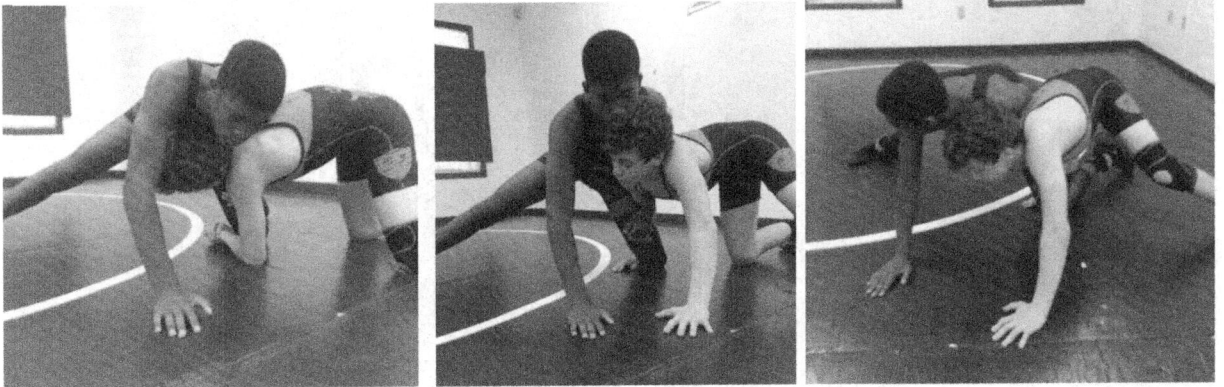

Turn The Corner & Limp Arm

As you turn the corner the man may have your arm secured with a tight Whizzer, to fully gain control you can off set your opponents Whizzer pressure by limping your arm down in a forward circular motion. Your opponent will lose Whizzer control and you'll come back full circle with the limp arm and use the arm to take hip control and come behind for your score.

Bring Leg to Outside for Greatest Leverage on the Drop

High leg back and withdraw the single to the outside slipping your lock to take control of his heel, secure the leg between your chest and thighs with trapping pressure. You don't get the sharp shoulder pressure as you do when you run the drop down the middle but you get tremendous leverage pressure by using the chest and leg pinch. To drop the opponent make him hop

Your opponent will try and work his leg to the inside for his best leverage, If he gets it there you can pull back and rotate back inward with your head coming back through to the outside, reach across and change to a double and lift below the hips and drive through for control

Finishes

Drive Across to a Double

With head inside your opponent may follow you with a hop towards you to keep balance when you go to withdraw for the drop. If he does simply drive across as he hops trapping both legs for a tight double leg finish.

Heave - Ho

With an outside leg single jack up the trapped leg with your far knee getting both arms under the leg simply step in making him hop back and then withdraw taking with leg high as you withdraw back.

Finishing With leg to the Outside

Pulling Outside Leg & Rotating In to a Double

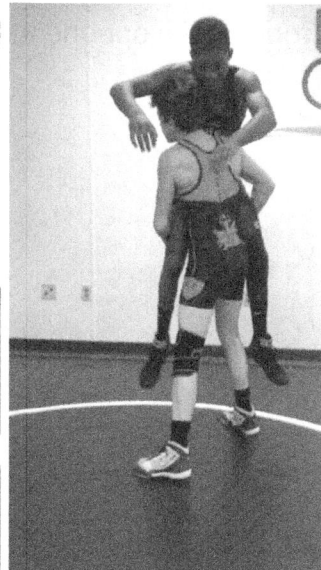

Pulling Outside Leg to a Front Trip

The front trip can be performed from an outside control position, once you have the leg pinched come up for an under hook keeping the other lock secured at the ankle. Take a cheat step planting down in front of your trip leg then lift your near trip leg high and across his leg tripping (above his knee so he can't hop over the trip). As you trip out his free leg punch your under-hook forward to get the maximal force of movement. As he drops get control

* High-Crotch To a Double

Slip By with a Rotation step - Switch to Double or Cross Ankle Pull -

The High Crotch is a pivoting maneuver that allows you to slip by your opponents arms. Offsetting his forward motion to deeply penetrate in on a leg attack. As your opponent pressures forward slip his arm by as you pivot on the inside foot - reach deep with the far arm coming through the opponents crotch then immediately switch pressure back towards the center of your opponents balance coming up and around with a double leg lift - dropping the opponent away from your head for the score

* Duck Under

Much like the high crotch using your opponents incoming pressure against him To create the opportunity duck under your opponents arm penetrating with a step in using the step and a pull on the far shoulder with your far arm hooking and pulling use also the back of the neck to pressure in and come behind to take control. You can then secure the waist and to clamp and drop the opponent with a knee block or a trip to the mat.

* Head Outside Single

Head Outside Single/Off Post, clear or slip by /Angle position/Quick lift

Take a deep penetration step letting your head come to the outside while reaching deep and high in the crotch with your lead arm. Let your outside arm secure the leg at the knee immediately begin pressuring into the opponents center of balance getting the angle and driving him toward his free leg. It is very important that you immediately get the angle and keep the angle that allows you to drive back towards your opponent's center, otherwise your opponent will be able to hook on to your hips and get the angle advantage to cross face and come around and score defensively.

Finishing Options Include

Trap Far Ankle

Head Outside on a Single Leg & Switching to a Double Leg

* Single Leg Sweep

Another maneuver that uses your opponent's forward momentum against him. Set by circling away from the leg that you are targeting. As the man follows anticipate his step while you are also setting your back leg to spring a shot towards his stepping leg Trigger your push foot as he is following and stepping to outside of the leg you are attacking. Penetrate in and hook elbow deep with your near arm while posting palm down for support on the mat with your far arm. Follow through - Hi-Legging back to turn the corner. As you turn the corner using the support of your posting hand on the mat, transition the post hand to snatch and hook the opponents ankle, come up to your feet securing a single with outside drop pressure.

Turning the Corner on the Single Leg Sweep - Key Points
Penetrate to the outside while posting with the outside hand for support - hook behind the knee and hi-leg around picking up the leg. Attack On his step as you load your back leg in a cocked and loaded position - spring your shot as he follows with an Outside Step Single - Hook your outside arm behind the knee of the leg you are attacking - with your inside arm post your hand to mat to support your weight and maintain an upright position as you turn the corner. Pivot behind with weight on your Lead penetrating Leg's knee, then high leg back with your trail leg, picking up your opponent's leg as you Turn the Corner.

* Fireman's Carry

Secure an overhook on the attack side arm, pivot inward stepping through with your outside leg while reaching deep and high in the crotch with your outside arm clamp down on the overhook and come to your side while firing upward with the arm in the crotch. Secure control popping your head out so that the man is unable to turn in as he hits the mat.

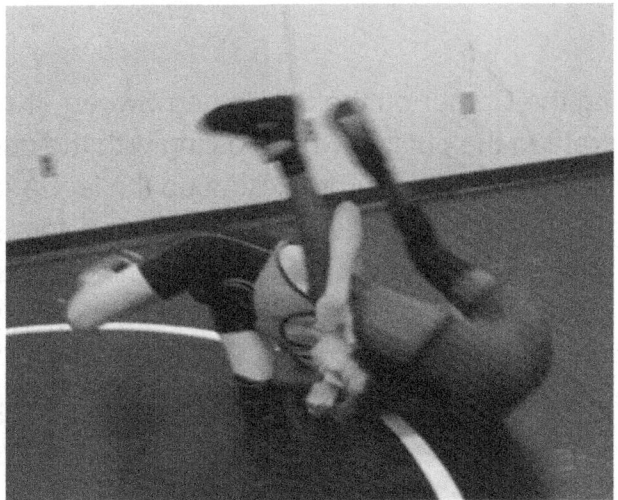

* Underhook Series

Take control with an Underhook while also securing inside head position. If you lose head control position regain it by working the back of your head back into inside position. With the under hook secured you can easily dictate your opponents movement and set up a variety of attacks.

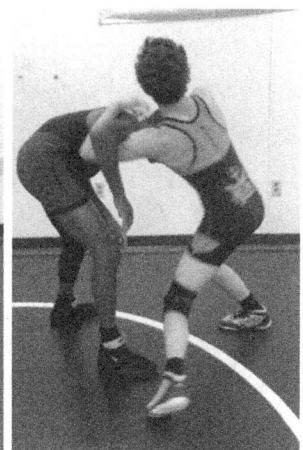

To an Ankle or Knee Pick

Use a circular motion to set up an ankle pick, as the opponent steps reach and trap with a hook behind his heel. Now change your direction with a drive forward pulling out the trapped foot as you drive.

Knee Pick

Same pressure as the Heel pick except hooking the back of the knee as your opponent steps and follows. Once trapped change direction driving through your opponent's center of balance, pulling the knee and pulling in with the Underhook.

Underhook & Snap The Head Down To a Front Head Lock

Man gets bent over or tries to back out. Snap down going heavy on his head, taking his nose to the mat. You can then clear his arm and come around to score.

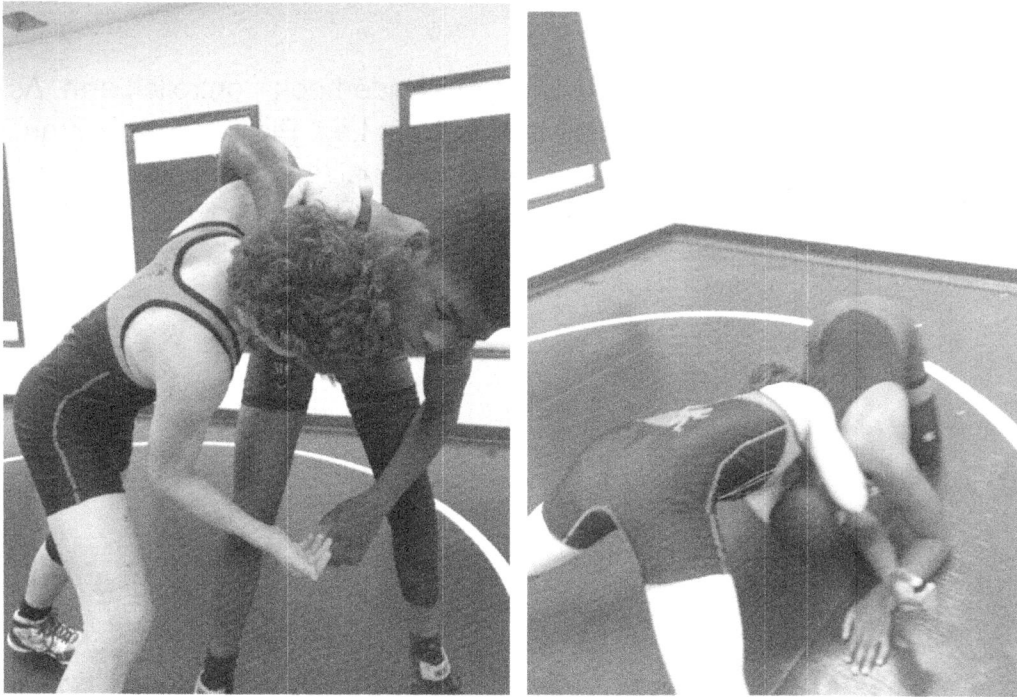

To a High Crotch coming back across for a Double Leg

When a man does not follow you can rotate inward with a hi-crotch reach then pivot around switching to a double leg lift

To a Near Single Snatch

Pressure in to your opponent's center of gravity with your Underhook Controlled arm. As you back his weight onto his far leg drop and snatch the Near Leg. Picking it up with an elbow deep two arm lock, securing the Single Leg with head inside and shoulder in the quadriceps pressure. Finish the single with the step and drop.

* The Over Under Series

Digging for Inside Control

Wrestlers are constantly fighting to gain the upper ground in the battle for Inside Control. This battle is called Pummeling. If you lose control on one side look to dig back with an Underhook on the other side, never giving ground where your opponent achieves a double Underhook position.

Over-Under Tie Up to a Head Lock Throw

With the overhook and the head inside - as your opponent steps back you have room to step and rotate your hips through while also locking your Underhook into a head and arm secured lock. Step the hips through pivoting in while pulling downward on the locked head and arm. The closer you can keep your feet together through the pivot the higher the pop will be to your opponent as you make the throw.

Over-Under to an Arm Throw

Pivot to the outside coming in with a hooked arm elbow deep. Rotate your hips through and pop your hips pulling downward on the trapped arm. Or use your outside leg to trip out the near leg as you pop your hips and pull downward on the arm.

Over-Under to a Trap Arm Near Leg Trip

An over-hooked arm can be trapped and clamped, once clamped step behind the trapped arm leg and trip forward and downward.

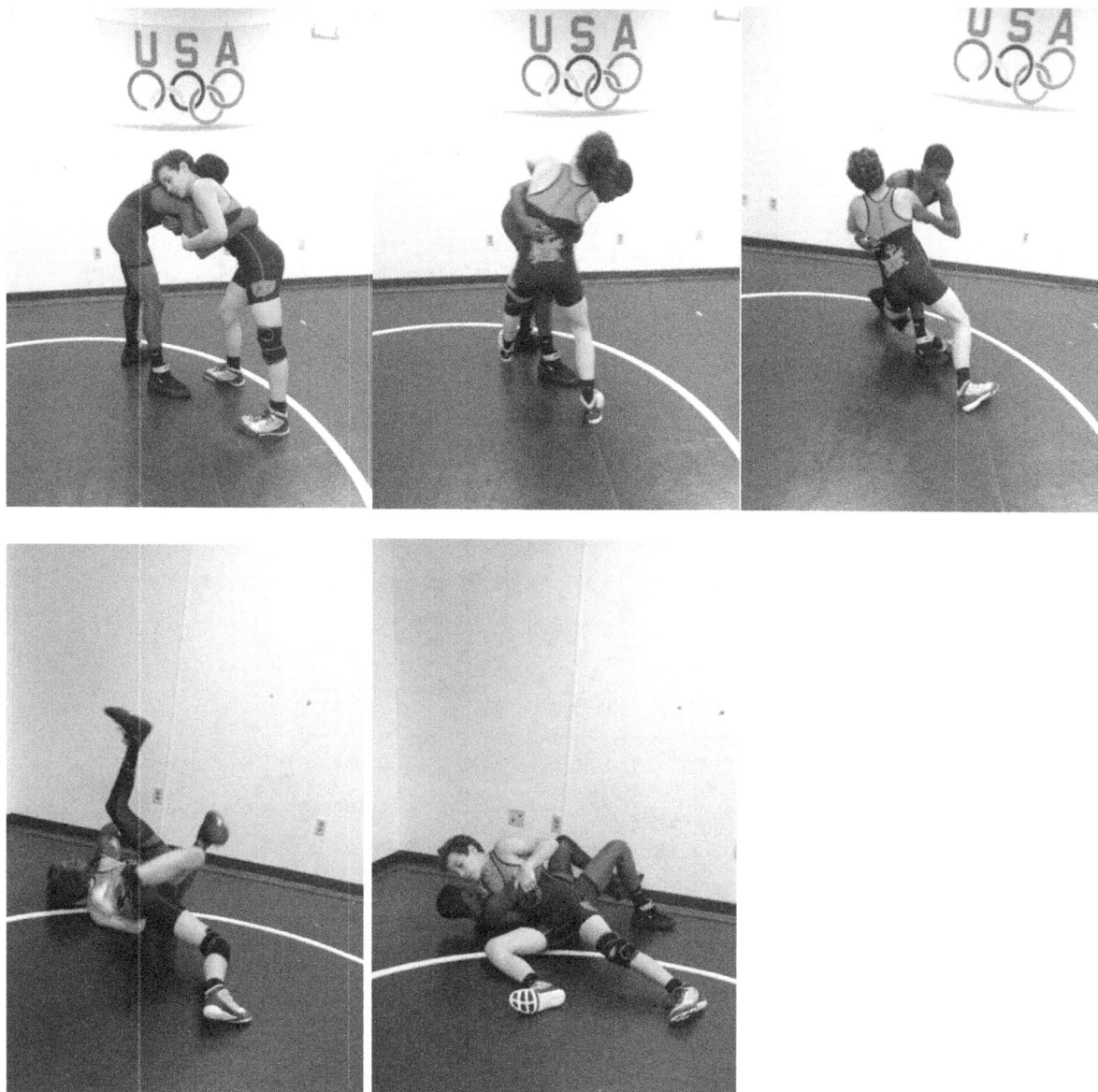

Over-Under to a Duck Under

As the opponent digs and pressures in - lower your level and slip your head through under his arm pit stepping through and pulling on the far over hooked arm to pull you around - secure his hips and trip down to gain full control.

Over-Under to a Fireman's Carry

When your opponent backs away - Rotate in on the over hooked side of the over under. Clamp and pop the fireman's

Over-Under to an Inside Trip

Bait the man to step forward - anticipate the step and come through with your overhook side leg hooking your opponent's leg then withdrawing the leg with your hook as you then drive and pressure through with your chest. Drop the opponent to his back and secure him with your weight on.

* Russian Tie Series

Collar Tie Shrug to a Russian

A maneuver that takes off your opponents collar tie. To initiate it, reach and grip your opponent wrist with your opposite side hand, shrug your head to the side and bump his arm with your near arm's bicep into your opponents triceps. Secure the arm with both hands (one hooked at the wrist the other at the bicep) now apply pressure on his triceps with your shoulder. Once you have secured the arm you can dictate movement and set up various attacks.

Russian Tie to a Near Single

You can bump the arm and trap a Near Single - Pressure in with your shoulder and dump him to the mat.

Russian Tie to Fireman's Carry

You can rotate in of your Russian into a Fireman's Carry. When your opponent backs his near leg away he has created an opening for you to rotate in on the over hooked side of the Russian Tie, as you rotate in reach deep in the crotch with the arm that had maintained wrist control on the Russian Tie. Once you are in deep on your knees clamp down on the over-hooked arm and pop the fireman's with an upwards thrust to the crotch and a forward motion going to your own shoulder. Pop your head out and finish with a pinning combination.

Russian Tie to an Arm Spin

Once you have taken off the opponent's Collar Tie and secured Russian Tie pressure, the opponent may withdraw his Lead Leg back, clearing the way for you to rotate in and around the secured Russian Tie arm. Once you have spun through you can maintain back arm pressure and bring the opponent downward.

Russian Tie to a Near Single Leg Snatch

Pressure in to your opponent's center of gravity with your Russian Tie controlled arm. As you back his weight onto his far leg drop and snatch the Near Leg. Picking up and securing the Single Leg with an elbow deep two arm lock, maintain head inside and shoulder in the quadriceps pressure. Finish the single with the step in - corkscrew downward withdraw step drop.

* Foot Sweeps

The Foot Sweep can be performed when you have secured Double Under-Hooks. Bait your opponent to brace and defend in the opposite direction of which you plan to strike. Pull downward on the opposite side that you want to attack, once you feel your opponent brace to compensate for your pull down, now shift all of your weight to your far leg - using a burst of hip and torque motion bring your opponents upper body towards your sweep side leg. Your sweep side leg should maintain its position as a blocking obstacle that your opponent's legs are forced to cross. With the right torque your opponent's weight should be off is feet as he is swept across your sweep/ blocking leg. Continue the movement as you knock his legs out with the sweep, following through to the mat as you continue with a near under hook pull-down and finish on top of your opponent, chest on chest.

Part II   Neutral Defense

PSU's John Hanrahan battles Perry Hummel (Iowa State) at NCAA National Tournament. Hanrahan came out on top 5-4.

* Fight Off Single Leg

When an opponent gets in on a Single Leg you must immediately push his head away as you insert a Whizzer around his near arm and insert downward pressure pulling your leg back and upward on your Whizzer hook to break his grip. Immediately work your controlled leg to the inside where your opponent will get less leverage to drop you.

Push his head away, pull up on the Whizzer and downward on the trapped leg. Make your opponent carry all of your weight and dictate short hops to keep him reacting and off-balance. With the correct pressure he does Not have Your Leg You Have His Arm.

* Head-Lock Trip off Single

Defending the single with the proper pressure will cause your opponent to become over-extended, opening him up for a Head Lock off a Far Leg Trip. Over-Hook a Head and Arm Lock, Cheat step over with your non-trapped leg and then slip your trapped leg to a Trip across your opponent's far leg, sweeping it out behind his knee as you also clamp and pivot your hips in throwing your weight into the Head-Lock. As you land sit up and through in to a tight Head Lock Sit Position.

* Fight Off Double Leg

To defend off a double leg shot square of and sprawl as the opponent begins penetration. Get your weight on and maintain pressure back in on the opponent - stop his hip power by getting his body extended and his head down. Once you have pressure on and his head down walk your legs back to break his grip, reach down or across to push down or drag his arm, with chest pressure on his back and his attack arm cleared, spin behind and score control.

* Lat-Throw off Double

If your opponent gets in deep on a Double Leg and you've missed the initial opportunity to fend off his incoming penetration with a Cross Face - Reach back around hooking the opponent's Lat. Maintain an over-hooked Whizzer with your near arm, step in and hook your inside leg for a trip.

Chin Whip option

* Block & Snap-Defending Shots

Superior position makes you the aggressor even in a defensive posture.

Defending Shots with Sprawls - Weight off of the front foot review

A good stance is the first element required to defend against an opponent's shot. If you've maintained weight on the back leg you can easily pull back your Lead Leg as your opponent begins to penetrate inward. Up-Block with your Lead Leg Protection Arm forearm to stop his incoming momentum - once you do, lower the boom to the back of his head, snapping his head - aim to out your opponent's nose in the mat. Once the opponent is extended keep the weight of chest on, reach down and transition the Snap side arm, under and across for an Under-Hook drag to the opponents tricep and use that hook to clear the arm off your leg and as a handle to drag yourself around and gain control.

Snap & Spin

* Head Snap to Pancake

After you block your opponent's shot with a block and snap down, maintain weight on with your chest. When the opponent goes to rear upwards let him come up while changing your snap arm to a cross face, bring the cross face up against him in an upward whipping motion while you maintain a Whizzer Hook on the far side. Once you've dropped him towards his back, sit your hips through, pulling up on the Over-Hooked arm and tighten the grip and the applying all of your weight on the opponent.

* Head & Arm Series

Head & arm - clamp & control

Once the opponent is extended keep the weight of chest on, reach down and lock a two on one Head and Arm lock. Further extended your opponent reach across and into a short drag.

Upon Blocking your opponents shot with a Snap Down or a Forearm Block, stay heavy on his head with your chest and shoulder, reach down and across his neck, locking up your opponents head and arm. Pull it tight by clamping your elbows while maintaining your head in his side. Reach for a Short Drag and spin behind.

* Head & Arm to Pancake

After blocking a shot, stay heavy on his head and shoulders, you feel the man come up come under with a cross face and assist him up with an upward hipping motion while maintaining a Whizzer-hook on the far arm. Once you've taken him over to his back finish with a Head Lock sit through.

* Head & Arm Shuck-By

If the opponent follows you while you begin circling with the Head and Arm Lock - Let him continue to go in that direction by unleashing the lock and rolling your forearm across his face, assisting him to continue going further and faster in that direction as you change directions and come back around to score control.

* Head & Arm to Cradle

As you begin to turn the corner with the head and arm secured in a lock, the opponent may brace, putting his knee up for extra support - if he does continue going in that direction bringing his head even closer to his knee, then slap on a Cradle lock - with your arms going in elbow deep at his neck and knee joints. Keep your head in the side for maximal control. Pressure across his body, slip your shoulder below his and drive him onto his back while maintaining your lock. As he hits his back keep your lock and settle your weight bring your head up and butt down, Keep your weight off your knees.

Man Sits thru - Roll Through and Clamp a Cradle

If the opponent sits through on your cradle. Don't panic, keep your lock and hip heist up into a Neck Bridge going along with your opponents roll and clamping him up on the other side. Remember once you've locked the cradle keep your head in the side, even as you roll through with a cradle. Finishing Head up and Butt down.

* Cement Job (Bull Dog) & Cement Mixer

Similar to a Pancake except that you have a Head and Neck Hook. When you feel your opponent rearing upward fire your under-hook arm high keeping it elbow to elbow as you go. Whip it over while keeping weight down with your other arm which will fall into a deep Half Nelson. Once you have dropped him to his back maintain weight on and settle his your Head up and Butt down.

You can also drop your opponent into a Head

Cement Mixer

Take the Head and Neck hook, as you drive the Under-hook arm up as in the Cement Job your opponent braces back down. As he does bring your hook arm back downward grasping his Lat, with the Lat hook and neck/chin hook begin to roll under the opponent in the direction he was pulling himself to. As you come out of the roll hip heist clamping your half nelson, that your neck hook will natural fall into and settle your weight.

Rolling Through with it - Man braces downward hook down on the Lat and roll him through.

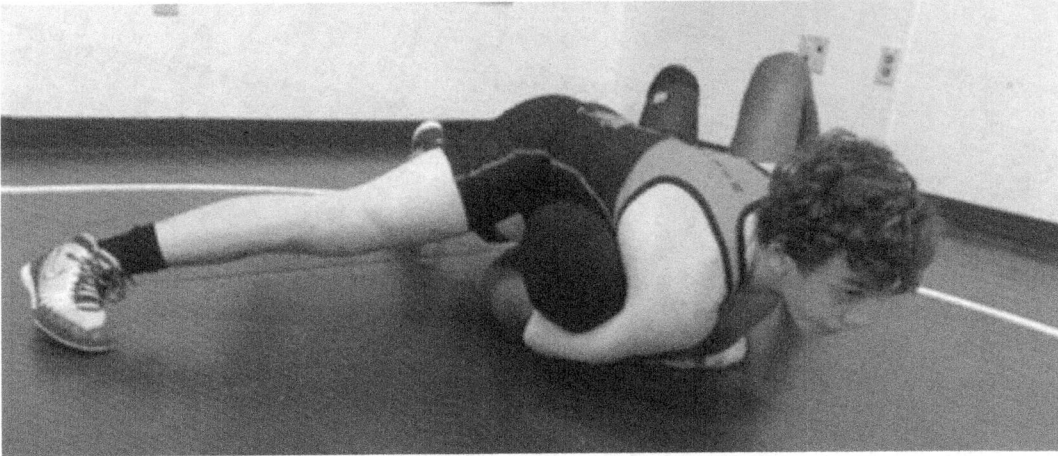

* Whizzer & Three Quarter Nelson

When your opponent gets in on either a Single or a Double you can Over-Hook and create Whizzer pressure. Over hook the attack arm hip in and drive pressure downward onto his trapped arm's shoulder.

Three Quarter Nelson

With the opponent's shot blocked and a Whizzer arm applied. Pressure downward with your free hand onto the head palm down. Reach up with the Whizzer arm and place that hand palm down onto of your other hand. You now have applied a 3/4 Nelson which exerts tremendous pressure. Keep coming around away from his extended arm and reach up and tug the hips down once you have dropped his neck to the mat. Keep coming around with your weight on and settle into a Reverse Half Nelson.

* Trap Head Tight Waist Hi-Leg

When an opponent shoots in on either a Double or a Single. Block the shot with a Whizzer and then push the head down and pinch it between your knees. Apply a Tight

Waist with your non-Whizzer arm- maintain your head pinch and drop to your side away from your Tight Waist arm. Once on your side Hi-Leg back to break his grip on your arm. Hip Heist and come up with Reverse Half Nelson.

Isolated Look - Tight Waist, Trapping the Head and Hi-Leg

* Trap Head - Spilatal

When the opponent shoots and you have him blocked, over-hook and pressure a Whizzer, push and trap the head between the knees, hook and lock the outside knee while also stepping in and hooking the inside knee with your near leg (stay knee joint deep with your leg hook and elbow deep with your arm lock on the leg).Now rollback pressuring upward on the back of your opponents neck with your hip flexor. Plant your free leg for support and settle with your hip flexed off the mat to maintain inward pressure on the opponent.

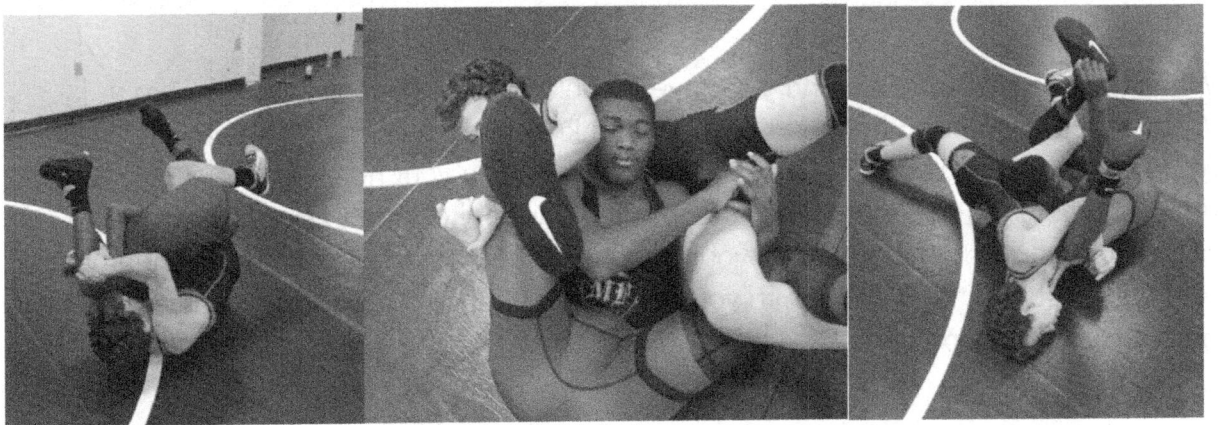

PART III TOP POSITION

PSU's Hanrahan takes top against University of Maryland's, Marlow. Hanrahan prevailed 25-3.

* Top-Set Position

Stand behind your opponent and wait until he gets set. When the official waives you on line your chest on your opponents mid back. Wrap your waist arm to the navel, palm side resting on the opponent. Take an elbow grip rest your near knee beside your opponent's thigh and raise your back knee up behind your opponent's hips.

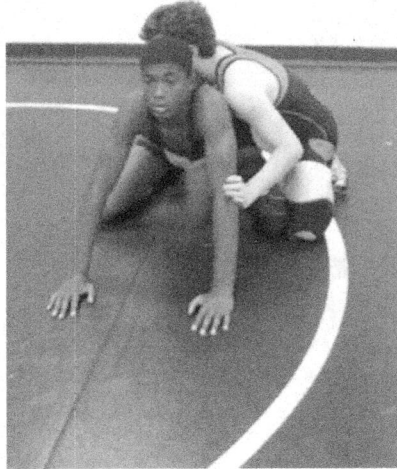

* Tricep & Ankle

On the whistle hook under and across with both arms hooking the far elbow and the far ankle. Position your chest to the side of the opponent's torso and drive across as you also pull in the hook elbow and trapped ankle. Once you have dropped the opponent to his side transition to a Half Nelson pinning combination.

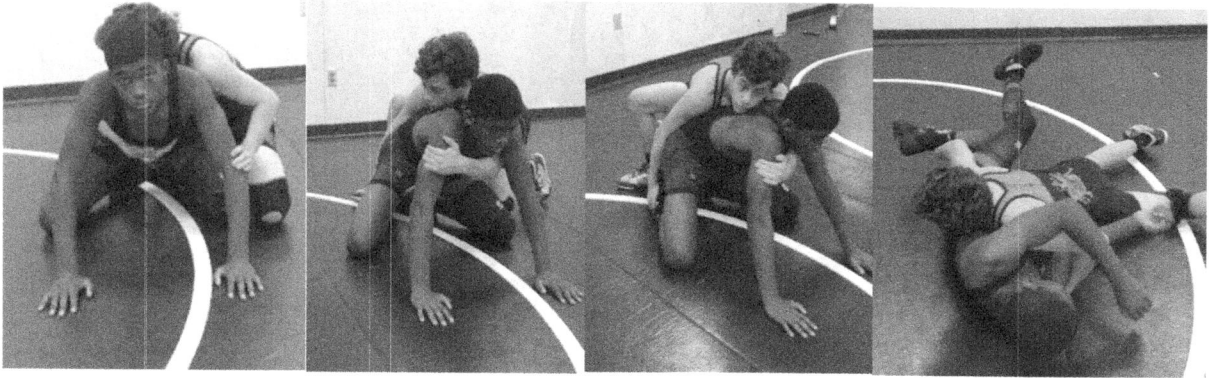

* Bump to Tight-Waist

Tight waist and chop the both the opponent's near arm and near thigh rolling him on to your thigh - then immediately come forward with your rear knee driving through your opponents hips, knocking him forward as you tighten a two on one lever grip to the arm of the opponent which you chopped inward. Once you have laid the opponent out with the rear knee follow through, transition your weight off your knees and pressure all of your weight on to your opponents back as you continue to hold his chopped arm in a two-on-one trapped position.

* Two on One Hi-Leg Turk

From the Bump to a Tight-Waist Breakdown with the chopped arm secured two-on-one and your full body weight pressuring down on the opponent - release the elbow grip side of the two-on-one - maintain tight wrist control - keep pressure on your shoulder down into your opponent - hi-leg over and pick up at the knee, step in and scoop a Turk leg hook, bring your heel high to make sure all the weight clamps the opponent onto his back. Maintain wrist control or come up and rake a Reverse Nelson across the opponent's neck.

* Two on One Tilt Series

From the Bump to a Tight-Waist Breakdown position with a two-on-one secured on the chopped arm, ride your opponent's hips up on to your thigh pinching and controlling his hips with your thigh and back knee pressuring inward. Use your two-on-one as a lever, tugging him over on to his back by pulling at the wrist side of the two-on-one, As you turn the man towards his back continue jamming your bottom knee upward and now use your back leg to jack him up by hooking your instep behind the crook of his far knee. Continue pressuring with your bottom knee and thigh, constantly adjusting to cradle his hips, offsetting his hip power. Continue to use the two-on-one trapped arm as a lever, steering your opponents torso in the opposite direction that he is trying to fight towards.

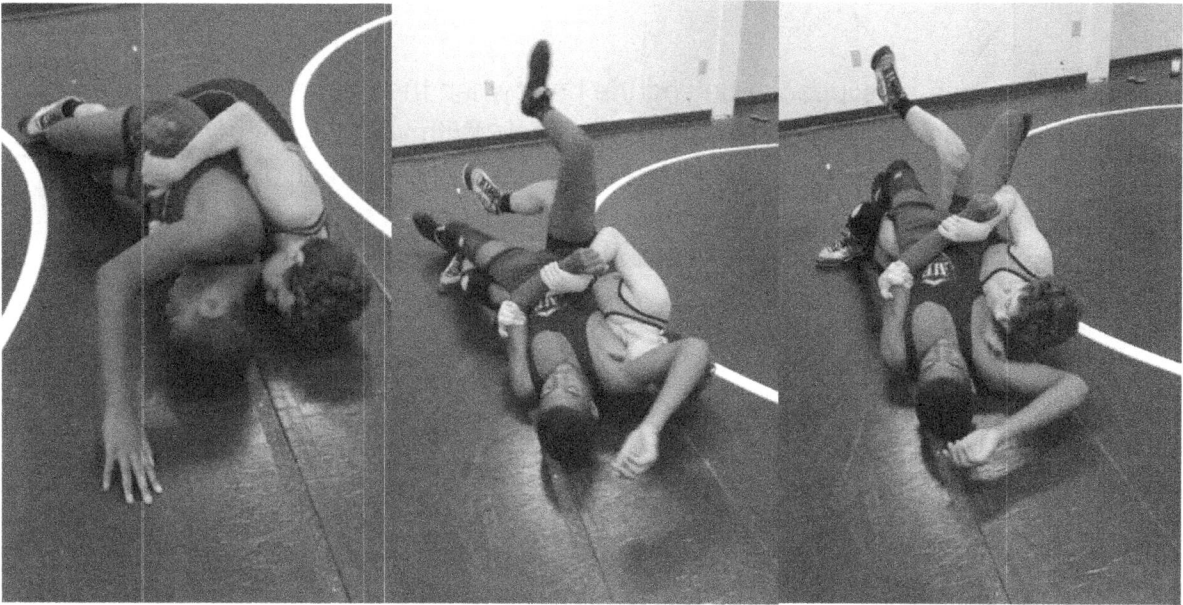

* Half Nelson

The Half Nelson can be slipped in behind the neck when the opponent is broken down flat. Snake your palm in behind the opponent's neck. With your weight on come out to the side and run your pressure into the man as you slip the half nelson deeper and deeper around the neck. As you are turning the opponent on to his back the Half Nelson should become elbow deep. Keep the weight off your knees and totally onto your opponent. Head up and butt down for maximal pressure.

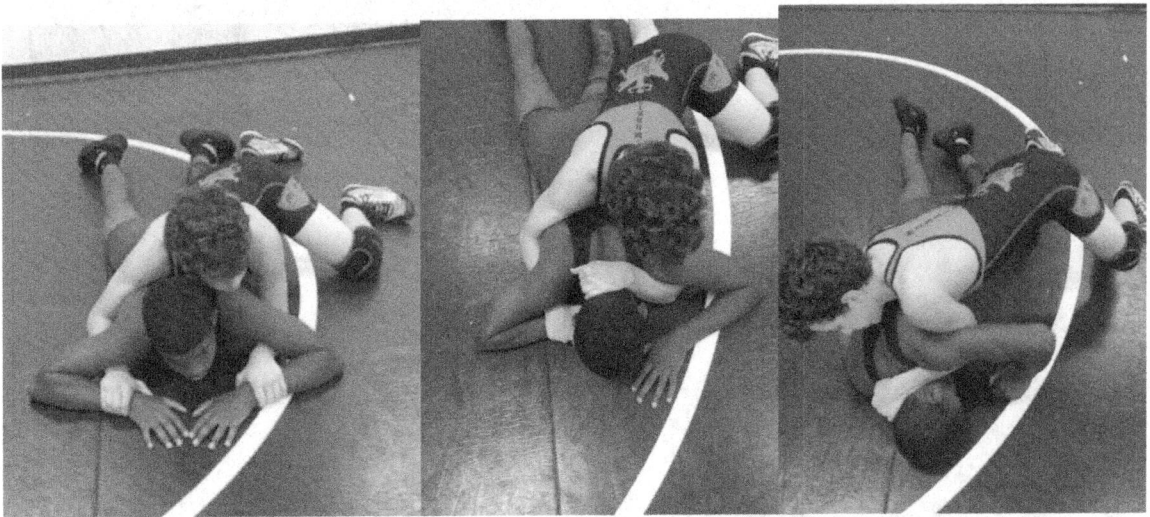

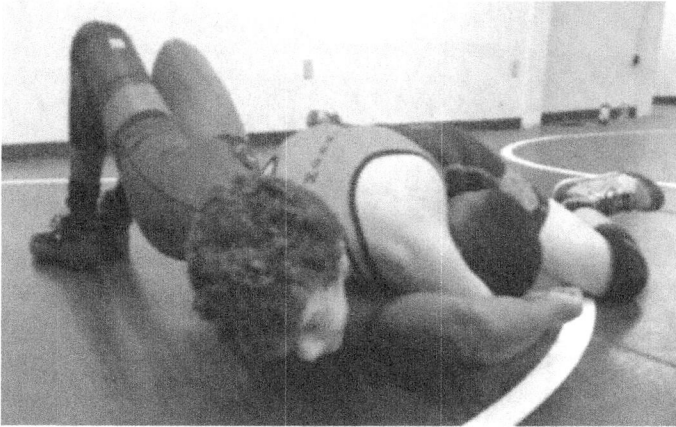

* Bar Arms

With the opponent broken down and wrist control on the trapped arm, peel back the opponent's free arm and slip a bar arm in at his elbow, as you start to run the bar arm release the wrist and post with your far arm palm down on the mat, driving the elbow of that arm into your opponents back. Begin driving the bar coming out front and driving your bar arm elbow to your opponent's ear. Settle with your weight on and maintain back point pressure.

* Bone to Bone

The Bone to Bone series is a single arm wrist control which also place the weight of your forearm against the immobilized arm. With your opponent broken down flat reach up and pull in your opponent's wrist as you pull the wrist inward and place the weight of your forearm onto the trapped arm you can safely come out to the side while maintaining weight-on pressure.

Turning Options include, hopping to your knees and pulling the wrist upward which forces the opponent to turn inward. As he does slip in a deep Half Nelson and pressure the body weight back on.

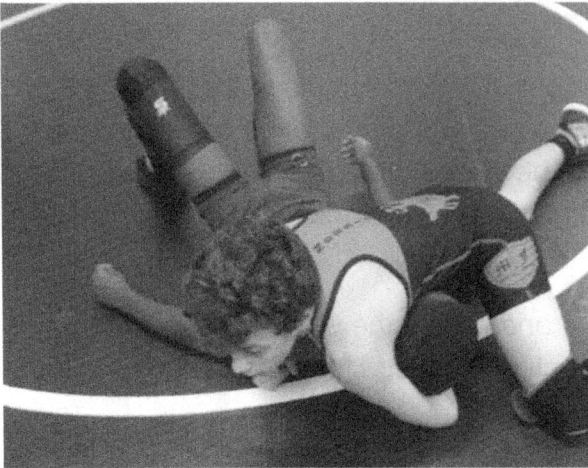

Other Angle

You can also come out to the side and slip a Bar Arm in as the wrist locked hand releases and goes to a Half Nelson - Turning your opponent now with a tight Bar & Half combination.

* Leg Series

To slip the Legs in pull up on the far ankles you jam the near arm forward allowing you space to step up and get your boot in through the crotch and drive it in deep until the toe is able to wrap and hold the calf. Take your upper body across the body and drive your elbow into his side - You now control your opponent with a Cross Body Ride. You can now pull up on the far ankle and break your opponent down.

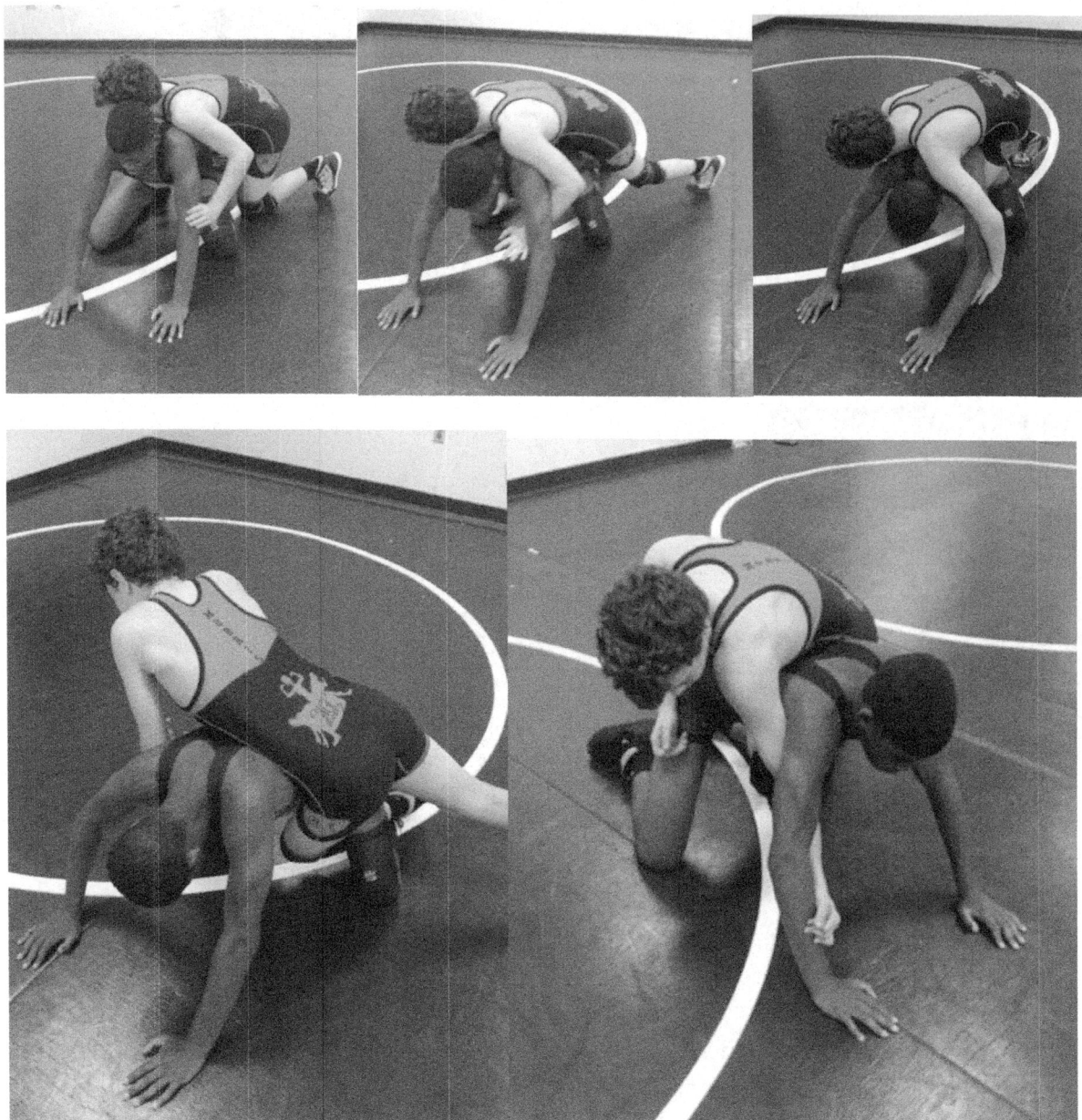

Guillotine

Look for his arm to post or come up to where you can take the arm with the elbow in the side arm slipping into a deep Reverse Half Nelson - Now you have a Guillotine and can move towards your own back - bringing your opponent to his back while maintaining full Cross Body control. The intertwined leg will continue to control the opponent's hip and enable you to maintain balance.

Leg Crank - with a Reinforced Half

You can also come up and slap on a Reinforced Half Nelson - drive your opponent's head downward while also pulling your opponent's torso towards the mat and exposing his back for points.

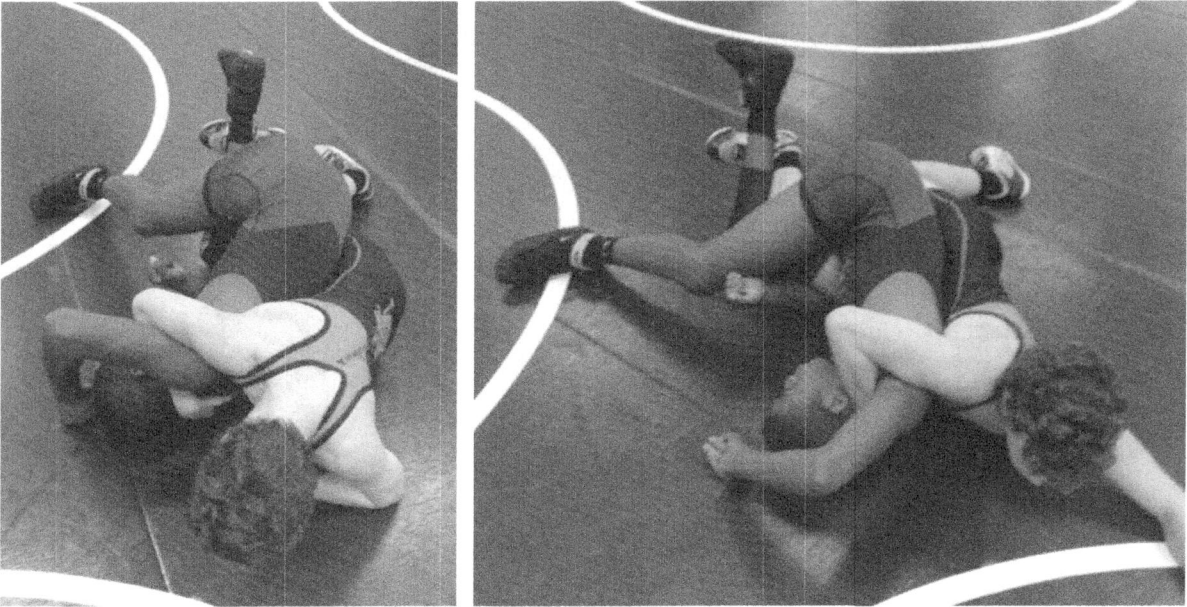

Leg Tilt Back

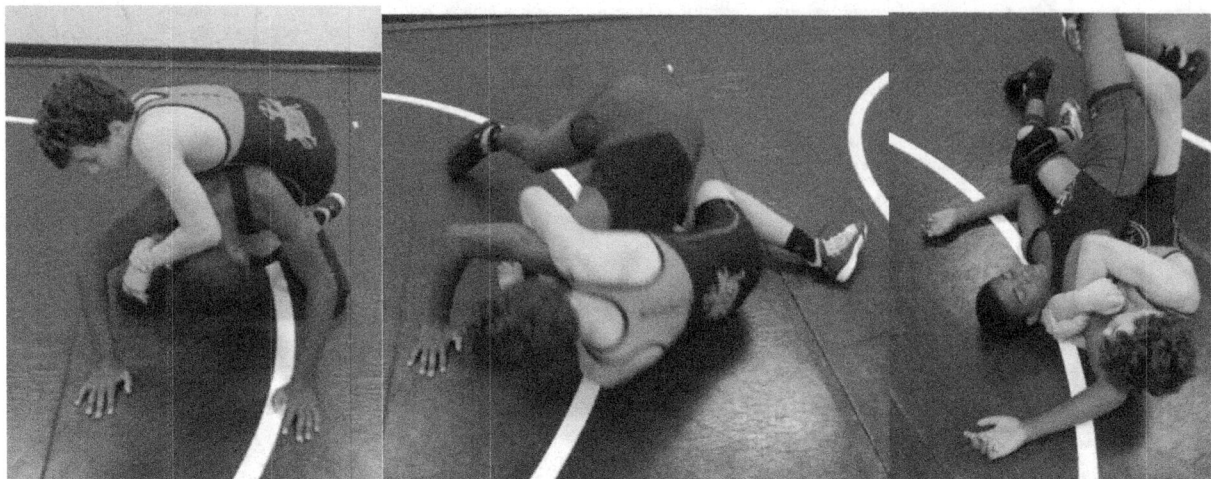

* Counter Stand-Up

When a man comes up with a Stand Up stay with his hips. Get a lock as soon as your opponent leaves his knees, preferably including an arm of his trapped in the lock, such as a two-on-one controlled arm. If you maintain superior hip position (having your hips in tight and positioned slightly below the opponent's hips you'll have maximum lift power). You can pop him just enough to sweep is near foot out and return him back to the mat in a laid out and controlled position.

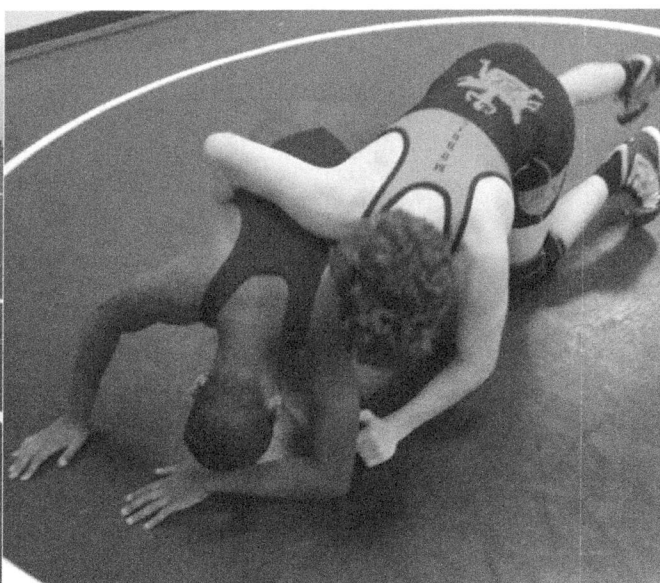

* Riding - Stay with the Hips

To key to becoming a successful rider on top is to learn to instinctually stay with your opponent's hips. Whether your opponent sits stands or switches a good rider stays with and controls the hips with clamps controls and fluid motion.

If the opponent tries to Power Roll /Granby, stay with the hips either with a strong enough clamp to stop the roll or by bringing your own hips along for the ride and maintaining superior control position.

Double Underhook Snap Back

When you are controlling the hips opportunities such as under hook snap backs will arise. Pressure in with double under-hooks then take the chin on one side withdrawal your hips and snap your opponent to his back. Lower your weight - chest on chest.

* The Claw & Spiral Ride

The Claw and Spiral Ride allows you to come out on your opponent, riding a little bit higher by maintain both thigh and neck pressure. Clamp an under hook in on the near side and a thigh pry in on the far side, spiral out in a way that allows you to maximize the pressure of both the holds.

The claw is similar but has a deeper reach which allows you to further control the upper torso. The claw will allow you enough control to roll under your opponent and create tilts and clamps that can be aided with a leg ride thrown in when needed.

* Cradle Series

Clamping a Near Leg Cradle

You can clamp a Cradle any time you are riding and you find that your opponent has made the mistake of bringing his head close to his knee. When you see it spin with the weight of your chest on your opponent's back, locking a clamp with one arm behind the neck and the other locking the leg. Both locks should go elbow joint deep on the head and leg targets. Once locked up keep your head in the side and drive across your opponent, slip back your shoulder below his shoulder and bring your head up and butt down to clamp at its tightest.

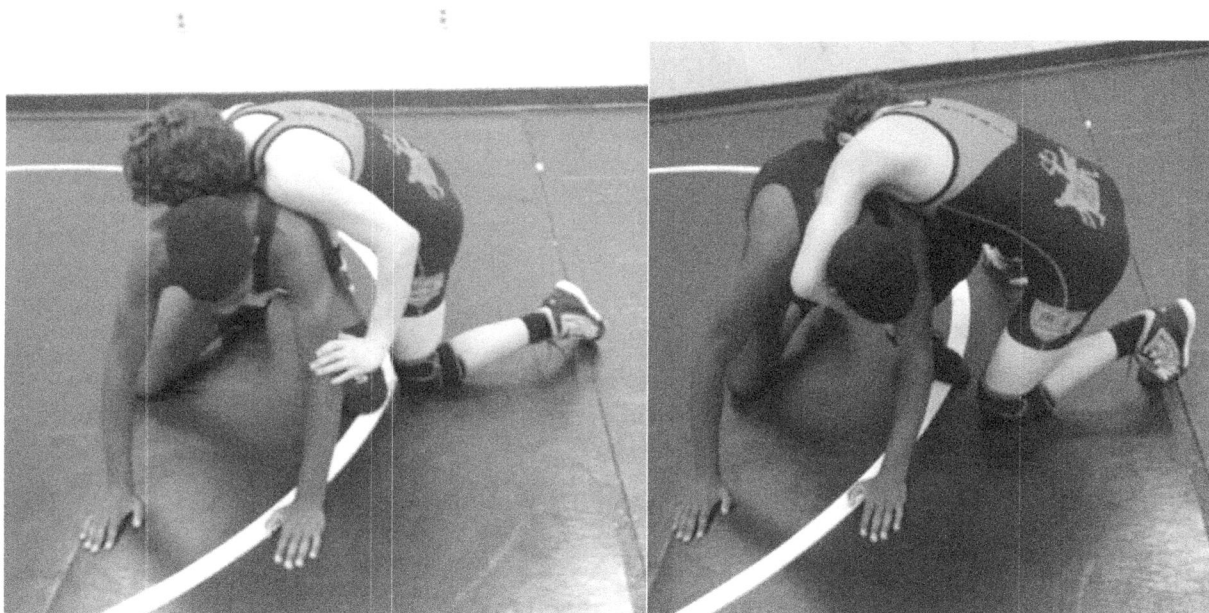

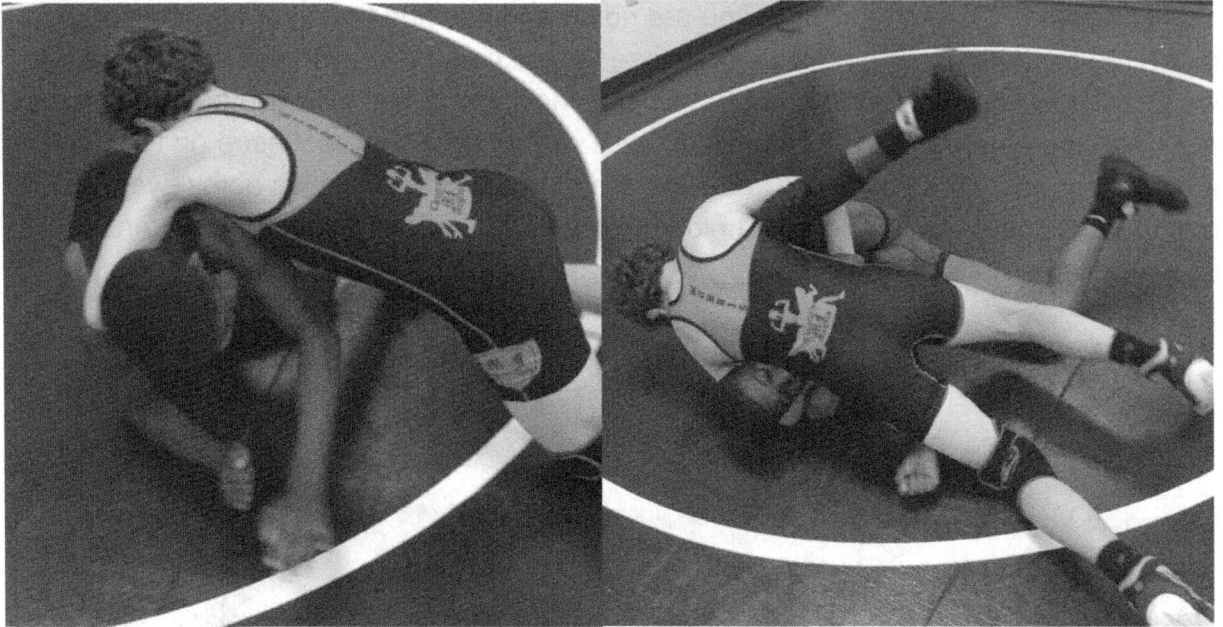

Cross Face Cradle

While riding crank the opponent's head towards his knee - once his head is near his knee clamp the cross face arm and leg cranking arm into a lock. Place your knee in the side and pull him back towards his back - you will go towards your own back in the process but maintain pressure and control, with your knee in the side.

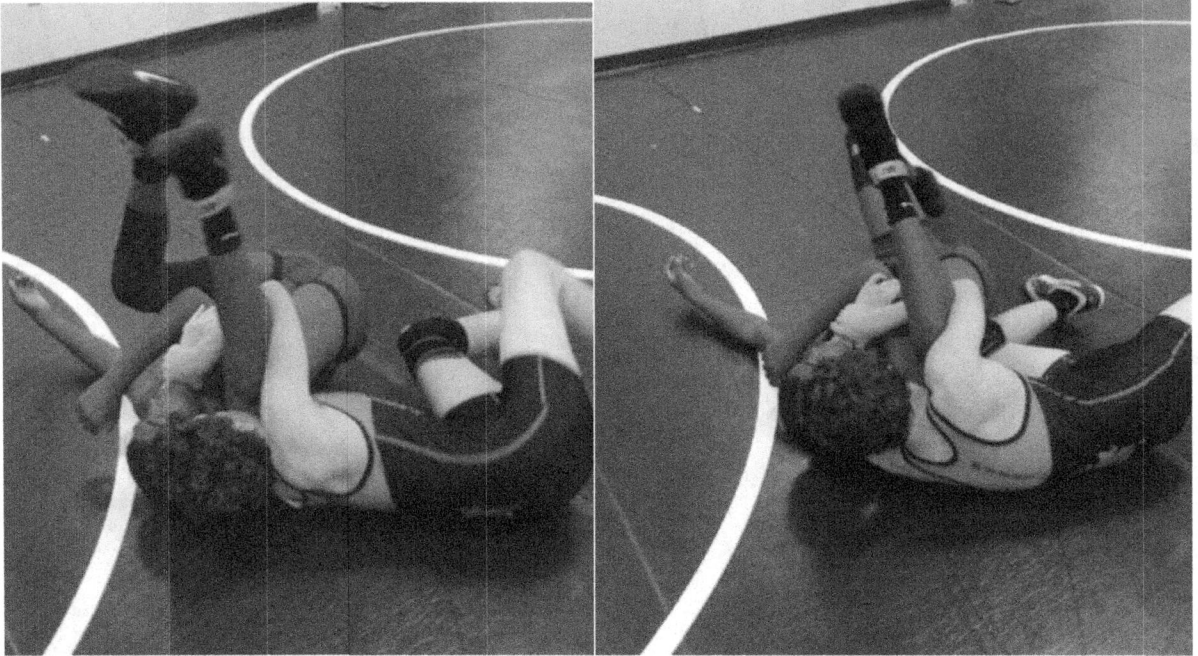

Sit & Roll thru Cradle

If the opponent sits through on your cradle. Don't panic, keep your lock and hip heist up into a Neck Bridge going along with your opponents roll and clamping him up on the other side. Remember once you've locked the cradle keep your head in the side, even as you roll through with a cradle. Finishing Head up and Butt down.

Part IV Bottom Position

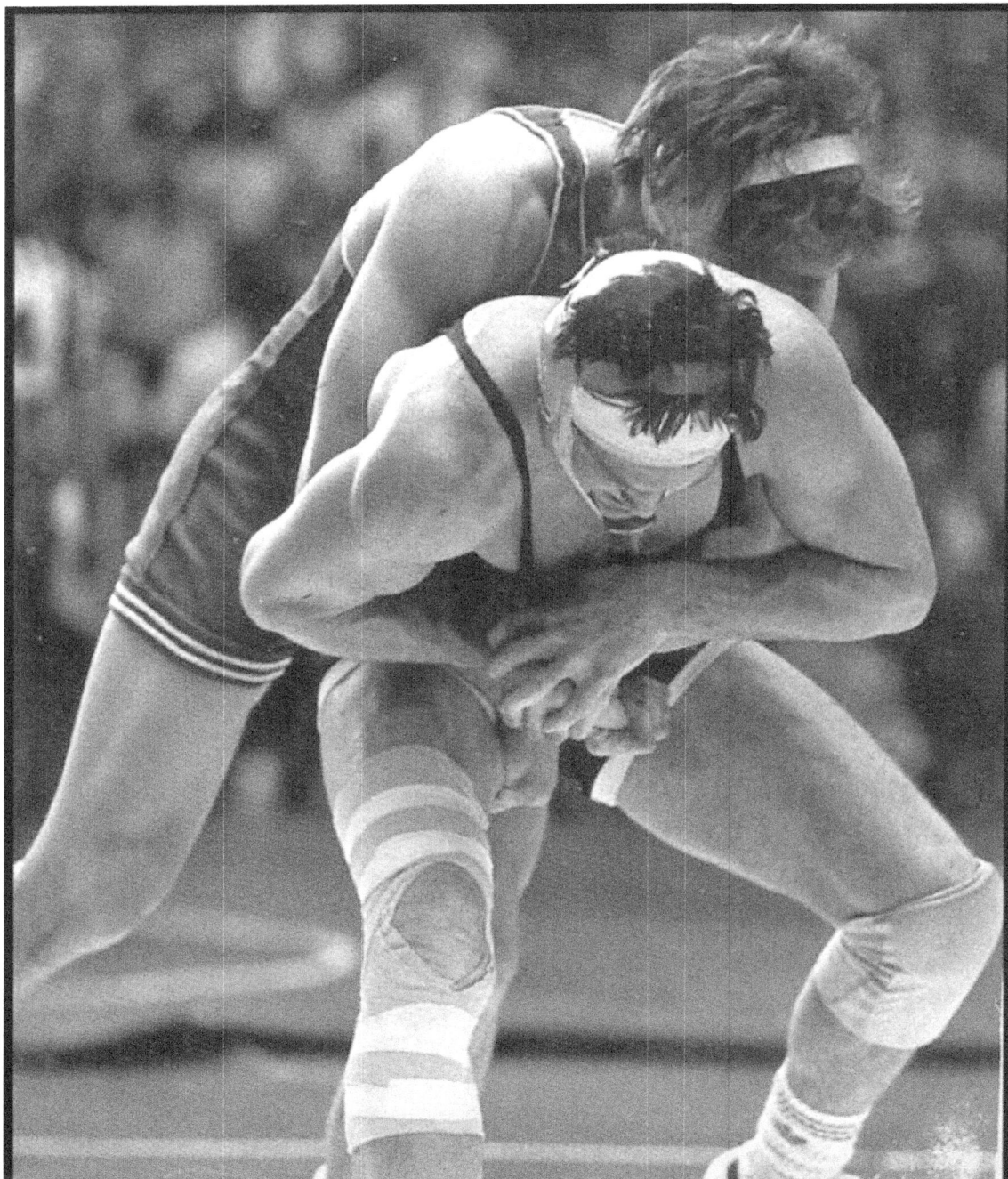

John Hanrahan escaping defending NCAA Champ Matt Reiss Hanrahan went on to win 13-6.

* Set Position

Line up by setting back on your feet with your laces down, bow your back in a cat back manner so that your opponent is forced to place his chest farther towards your lower back (allowing you more ability to fire your upper body back in to the opponent on the whistle) Check your position - be able to lift your hands without falling forward

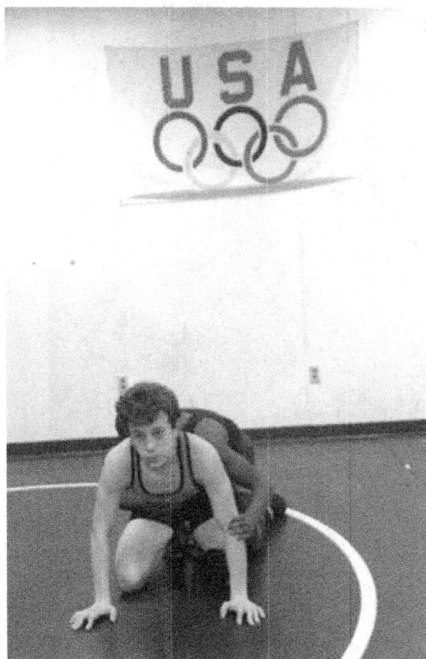

* The Stand Up

The key to a successful Stand Up is the ability to explode your hips off the mat with enough pressure back into the opponent to offset his forward pressure. Once you fire upward with the knees coming off the mat you can then get a foot out and continue driving back into your opponent. Elbows should maintain in inward position, sealing off any possibility of your opponent's ability to insert Under-Hooks.

Stand Up & Cut Out

Aim to knock your opponent over if possible. Begin with the attitude that you will exert nothing less than all out explosive pressure on the whistle. It gets much harder to escape if you wait. Envision yourself in a tank of water, get out quick, the longer you stay down there the less oxygen you will have, carrying your opponents weight on your back can sap your strength and burn up your oxygen.

As you explode up seal in the elbows, get a foot out, continue driving back into the man, get a two on wrist control, post it down and raise a cut back arm and pivot inward while maintaining pressure back. Once you've cut and face your opponent immediately position your stance for an attack.

Cutting Out

While continuing to pressure back into your opponent post his wrist downward using a two on one grip. Raise up with the arm on the opposite side of the wrist post - in a downward corkscrewing motion, while continuing to pressure back pivot inward and face your opponent. Immediately readying yourself in a stance to defend or attack.

* Sit Back Series

Swish your ankles to the side - sit back into your opponent sealing your elbows to your side to prevent being under-hooked.

* Sit Back to a Cut Out

A good sit back gives you the same type of pressure back into your opponent as a stand up. While continuing to pressure back into your opponent - look to cut out and escape. Post his wrist downward using a two on one grip. Raise up with the arm on the opposite side of the wrist post - in a downward corkscrewing motion, while continuing to pressure back pivot inward and face your opponent. Immediately readying yourself in a stance to defend or attack.

Turn In

Swish your ankle to the side, sit back into your opponent, gaining wrist control. If space is created by the opponent riding loosely, turn down on your non wrist control side elbow as a post, continue with wrist control and turn all the way under the wrist controlled arm - dropping your head under and coming out the back side. Immediately come behind the opponent securing hip control for the reversal.

*Sit Back to a Switch

Swish your ankles out, sitting back into your opponent. As you get to your sit reach back over your opponent's arm and into his crotch, this arm is now your lever and will provide downward pressure onto your opponent's shoulder as you bring your hips outward, driving your opponent's head towards the mat. Now pivot your hips and come around, converting the switch pressure arm into a leg pull to assist in pulling your body around, turning the corner and gaining control of the reversal.

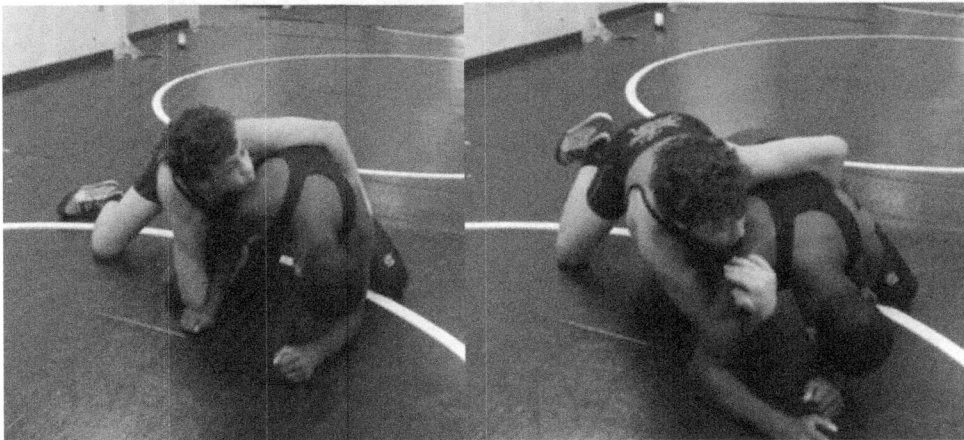

*Sit Back to a Power Roll/ Granby

Sit back pressuring into the opponent gaining wrist control. When the opponent continues to put pressure back in to you, step your non-wrist control side foot across, transfer all your weight to this foot which is now your "push foot", spring off this foot, tucking your chin to the chest and driving your hips up and over into a flying roll as you also maintain wrist control, throw your other arm across your chest to perpetuate the roll momentum. Land maintaining wrist control - come around and secure the hips for reversal control.

* Standing Power Roll /Granby

A strong sit back with pressure in from your opponent may bring you right to a stand position. With wrist control and the opponent driving in, step your push foot across and fire into a standing power roll - tucking your chin to the chest and driving your hips up and over into a flying roll as you also maintain wrist control, throw your other arm across your chest to perpetuate the roll momentum. Land either maintaining wrist control and coming behind or many times you may lose wrist control because the G-forces of the Roll - Simply roll fully out getting your escape, turn in and immediately face your opponent in an offensive stance.

* Power Roll /Granby to a Peterson

If your opponent follows on your roll, come through the crotch with your non wrist control arm. Instead of coming around behind continue rolling towards your back while bringing your opponent with you with your wrist and crotch trap. As you roll through your opponent will be under you on his back while you are on top of him in a controlled wrist and leg hold - called a Peterson. Continue to keep your weight fully on your opponent (butt off the mat), and control for back points.

* Fight Off Half Nelson & Off Your Back

When you feel an opponent begin to slip in a Half Nelson immediately look up and away from the side the Nelson was inserted - while also using your near arm to reach up to grasp and pull down the extended fingers of the inserted Nelson. You now have gained wrist control and can continue bettering your position by sliding one knee up and getting your hips back under you for a pressure back sit position.

If your opponent turns you to your back in a half nelson you have got to bridge and knife your hand your opponent's chest and your chest. Belly down as you knife your hand through and build back to a base with your head up.

* Leg Counters

To fight off the Leg Ride pressure back in enough to get one arm hooked under the opponents inserted Leg. Continue pushing back, bringing the hooked Leg up high to your shoulder, driving the hooked Leg arm towards your ear as you scoot the hips out and Come Out The Back Door.

Roll Out of Legs

Another way to escape Legs is to Roll through with your opponents inserted Legs. Raise up to a Tripod step the trapped leg foot in front of the other, tuck your chin to the chest and drive into a power roll. Once the man goes to his back Hip Heist quickly and maneuver your hips so that you now have a Leg control position. Come up across the opponent's racking a cross face while maintaining Leg and Hip control.

Catch The Leg Coming In - Come Out The Back Door

Escaping a Crab Ride

Fighting out of Legs from the Crab Ride position is much like escaping with your Cut Through from the Stand Up position. Gain two on one control, post the controlled wrist downward, raise up a Cut Through arm and cork screw down ward while Hip Heisting to face your opponent Chest on Chest.

You may even be able to catch the opponent's neck with your Cut Through arm and go into a Cradle or Head Lock to complete the reversal with a pinning combination.

Cut In Chest to Chest Option

Head Hunter Option

* Bar Arm Counters

To fight off the opponent's Bar Arm, reach out with your non Barred arm and place your hand over top of your Bar Armed hand. You now have increased your arm strength by two - Use your two on one arm strength to pressure your body back, bringing a knee up under your hips and driving into his Bar Arm pressure. Once you have neutralized the pressure look for a Turn In and come behind.

* Fight Off Back

From a Half or Reverse Nelson

Fighting off the back is no easy task. If you are trapped on your back you must immediately bridge up to avoid the fall. Insert your arm with your palm down on your on chest working the arm between yours and the opponent's chest. Once you have your arm working in, Punch it through, and while also Hip Heisting to Belly Downward. Work yourself back to a base with your head up. It takes a Never Say Die attitude to fight off the back but you can do it and turn the match around, never give up.

Escape when Trapped in a Tilt

When trapped in a Tilt, work to gain control of the opponent's knee that is jacking inward and controlling your hips. Push downward on the jacking knee and hop your hips over the opponent's leg, once you've got your hips out of his control, break the wrist and or two on one control of your arm and scoot out. Turn back into the man with a Cut Through or Turn in and attack back for Reversal control

Part V Mindset of a Champion

Penn State Wrestling - John Hanrahan, Two-Time NCAA All American, Two-Time Conference Champion. Finishing his career with Most Wins in Penn State's history (108) and inducted into the Eastern Wrestling League Hall of Fame.

* Mindset of a Champion - I CAN WIN

As a young AWN Freshman All American collegiate wrestler, I lost a heart breaking first round match at the National Championships my Freshman year, my coach immediately gave me some good advice. Coach let me know that I could either go sulk or relive my first round match for the next three days of the competition, or I could take this opportunity to gain an invaluable insight by studying the individuals who will come out as the Champions of this annual gathering of 350 battle hardened American wrestlers. I took his advice and used my competitor credentials to study up close, the common traits of the wrestlers who separated themselves from the hundreds of others. The ones who emerged as the Champions, one in each of the ten weight classes.

What I soaked up over the next few days of the tournament, enabled me to begin emulating those traits and return over the next few years as a highly decorated NCAA All American competitor, who even upset a few defending National Champions along the way.

I sum up the Mind Set of the Champion as the I CAN WIN formula:

Intensity

Confidence

Attitude

Never Say Die

Will

Intestinal Fortitude - GUTS

No Doubt

"I" is for Intensity. You can see it in the eyes of a champion, they are focused and already have the end result in sight. They take on the challenges that confront them in a workman like manner, never wavering from their purpose. Champs thrive on the intensity of competition, and climbing to new levels of achievement.

"C" is for Confidence. Every Champion I've observed carries himself with an air of confidence. Not to be confused with cockiness. They are what they are; and that's ready to beat you any way they have to. They don't look ahead dismissing the immediate challenge that is in front of them in an over-confident manner. They take one match at a time, and enter the circle of competition fully focused and confident.

"A" is for Attitude. Attitude is everything, sure champion's get hurt and have set backs, but their attitudes and how they deal with the obstacles are what separate them from the majority. You can have an attitude, that "I'm going to beat you", and still maintain high standards of sportsmanship.

"N" is for Never Say Die. A great coach taught me that every competitor is subconsciously looking for a reason or an excuse to lose. The going gets tough and very uncomfortable in the heat of battle, human nature may tell you to just pack in and go home, back to a nice comfortable place. At Penn State, we called it finding our opponent's "off button" you can feel it when it happens. Great champions do not have an "off button", they possess a Never Say Die attitude and refuse to quit or let up. They remain relentless in pursuit of victory and use every moment of the clock to make it happen, they never coast on a lead or let up or quit when behind. They will not rest or look for comfort in anything less than victory.

"W" is for Will. This is where the bulk of the traits are derived from. Do you have the Will to win, have you invested enough Sweat, tears and hard work to know that you deserve nothing short of victory. A champion cannot be denied of the thousands of hours of training and extra effort that have gone into their quest for greatness. They have paid the price and enter the arena to simply cash in their chips, and take home what they have worked so hard for. The Will to win becomes engrained in the Champion from the investment he has made in thousands of hours of hard work and sacrifices.

"I" is for Intestinal Fortitude - Guts. Champions are not front runners they do what it takes to "come back" when they get behind. If they get caught in a move or if an official's call does not happen go their way, they don't panic, lose focus or break up. They dig deep and derive a measure of Intestinal Fortitude to "Gut Out" a victory. No matter what, a true Champion will never quit.

"N" is for No Doubt. Champions do not fall in to the trap that the majority of competitors do. That is to fill your head with doubt. They do not use the word "can't" as often as others. Great Champions have already envisioned where they want to be.

* Journey of a Wrestler From Boys Club to World Champ

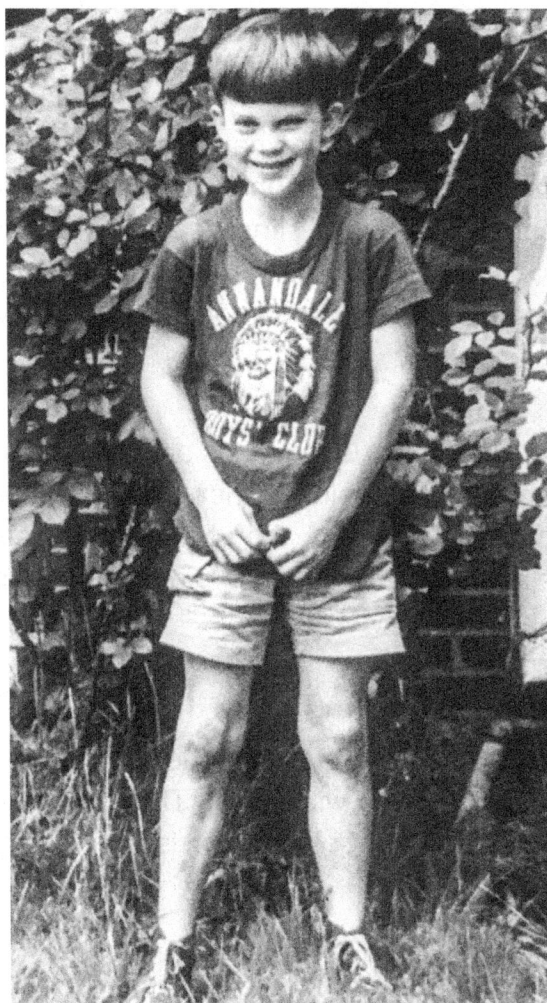

First year boys club wrestler john Hanrahan, second grade.

First high school match, Falls Church HS varsity 112 lber, John Hanrahan finishes under the spotlights in a tie.

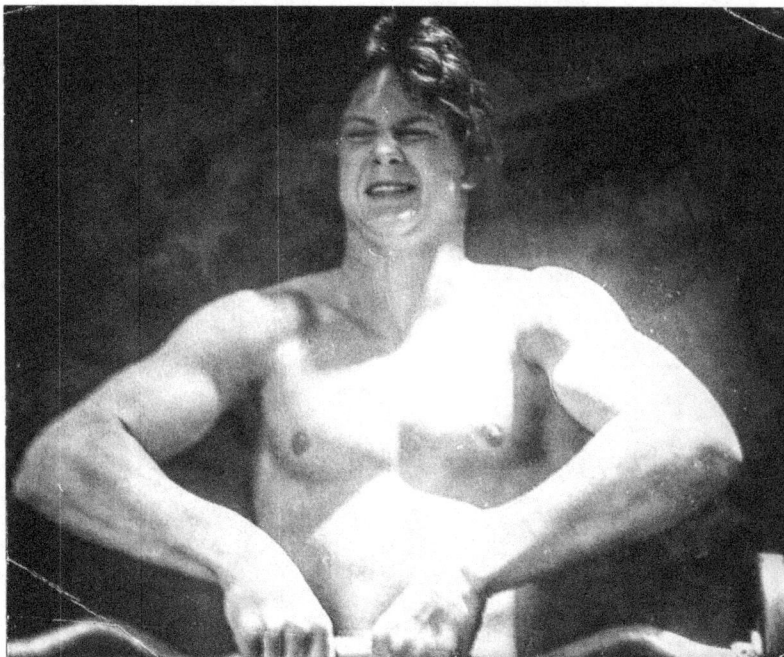

Post freshman season, HS wrestler john Hanrahan, lifting to get stronger and working to fulfill his goal of multiple state titles.

Virginia State Championship

10th grade wrestler John Hanrahan with Olympic Champ Dan Gable at the 1976 Olympic Games in Montreal. Hanrahan was on a Jr Olympic youth team that went on to compete in East Germany and Poland.

High school senior John Hanrahan competing at USWF HS Nationals in Iowa City, IA.

Penn State Freshman wrestler John Hanrahan, competing at his first NCAA Championship. Amateur Wrestling News named Hanrahan as the top freshman in the nation at his weight class.

1978-79 All-Star Freshmen Wrestlers

	First	Second	Third	Fourth	Fifth	Sixth	Seventh	Eighth
118	Don Cuestas, Cal Poly	Jim Pagano, William & Mary	Gary Bohay, UCLA	Brad Anderson, Brigham Young	Khris Whelan, Missouri	Matt Oddo, Auburn	Jeff Bean, Lafayette	Adam Cuestas, Oregon
126	Derek Glenn, Colorado	Don Reese, Bloomsburg	Harlan Kistler, Oregon	Pete Schuyler, Lehigh	Don Winter, UW-Parkside	Jim Lord, Iowa State	Gary Lefebvre, Minnesota	Bob Rury, Penn State
134	Darryl Burley, Lehigh	Lewis Sondgeroth, Colorado	Bill Nugent, Oregon	Mark DeMoo, Syracuse	Jeff Hardy, Ohio	Steve Cifonelli, Temple	Jerry Kelly, Okla. St.	Doug Calhoun, Upper Iowa
142	Andre Metzger, Oklahoma	Chris Catalfo, Florida	D. J. West, Northern Colo.	Brad Perry, Clemson	Gary Waller, UT-Chatt.	Russ Campbell, Weber State	Steve Roberts, Slippery Rock	Larry Luttrell, Northern Iowa
150	Steve Greenly, Bucknell	Matt Skove, Georgia	Tom Pickard, Iowa State	Ken Gallagher, Northern Iowa	Fred Worthem, Michigan St.	Bob Eon, Rhode Island	Frank Castrignano, N. Car. St.	Dave Millay, Utah
158	Ricky Stewart, Okla. St.	Mark Schultz, UCLA	Kevin Benson, Portland St.	Gregg Stensgard, N. Dakota St.	Jon Lunberg, Augustana S.D.	Steve Bassetto, Florida	Darryl Henning, Ft. Hays	Mark Granowski, Eastern Ill.
167	John Hanrahan, Penn State	Dale Walters, Air Force	Jim Hall, Oklahoma	Joel Davis, West Virginia	Tim Morrison, Messiah	Phil Herbold, St. Cloud	Keith Foxx, Arizona	Brett Stamm, Wheaton
177	Curt Lock, Marquette	John Bliss, Washington St.	Luke Draper, Washington	John Dougherty, Syracuse	Roy Martinez, Okla. St.	Jim Trudeau, Minnesota	Bill Ameen, SIU-Carb.	Joe Roth, John Carroll
190	Edgar Thomas, Oklahoma	Mike Mann, Iowa State	Joe Wade, Bloomsburg	Ed Mayers, Navy	Paul Gifford, Fairmont St.	Brad Moseley, Missouri	Terry Mensink, N. Dakota St.	Chris Johnson, Georgia
Hwt.	Steve Williams, Oklahoma	Glen Quakenbush, Arizona St.	Rick Passerotti, Bucknell	Mark Sullivan, Ohio State	Dave Armstrong, Temple	Craig Newberg, Ball State	Paul Finn, N. Caro. St.	Bruce Baumgartner, Indiana State

Founder of the Penn State 100-Win Club: John Hanrahan finishing his career at Penn State as the first in the school's history to surpass the century mark in victories.

Competing for the NYAC John Hanrahan was able to represent the USA medaling in international events.

In 2016 John Hanrahan fulfilled his lifelong goal of becoming a UWW World Champion. In Walbrych Poland he defeated legendary 10x UWW Veteran World Champ Willem Putter (RSA) in the gold medal match. Never give up your dreams, hard work will make them a reality.

United World Wrestling Gold Medal ceremony, Walbrych Poland.

ABOUT THE AUTHOR

John Hanrahan is a UWW Veteran World Champion. He competed at Penn State University where he was a 2-time NCAA All American, 2-time Conference Champion and 4-time place-winner. Other international medals include Canada Cup bronze and NYAC International 2-time gold. In high school Hanrahan was the USWF Jr. National Championship runner-up, AAU National Championship runner-up and 2-time Virginia State Champion and 3-time place-winner. He finished his Penn State career as the first in the school's history to surpass the 100 Win mark and has been inducted into the Eastern Wrestling League Hall of Fame. His NCAA coaching experience includes; grad assistant coach at Penn State, head coach at Fordham University and as an assistant coach at American University. He was named as the USA national Dream Team coach for the 2017 Pittsburgh Classic. He is an acclaimed former Hollywood Trainer and Certified Strength & Conditioning Specialist. His fitness web site is PrivateTraining.com and his author's web site is JohnHanrahan.com

Special thanks to our demo-wrestlers Marley Washington and Josh Noble

Made in the USA
Coppell, TX
15 December 2023

26145745R00090